Entertainment

A letter from the Author

Hello,

Welcome to **Entertainment**!
Entertainment means having fun. Enjoying yourself. Being happy. This depends on age, and personal tastes. What entertainment do older people like? Or kids? And how about the differences between you and your friends? To what extent does entertainment depend on fashion? Maybe on advertising, too?

Of course, some people like to be the entertainers. Others prefer to be the audience. And it changes all the time.

In 'Entertainment', we look at some different types of entertainment: music, films, circuses, festivals. We explore them in different ways. We ask questions about them. We discover connections between old and new forms, and between old and new audiences.

We also look behind a few film titles, types of music and groups of musicians. There are often extra things to discover about them.

We examine an exciting music project in the Amazon – involving young people, an inspirational teacher, and a determination to overcome problems.

Entertainment changes all the time. Things go in cycles: some of last year's hit films will still be here in the future. Others will disappear completely. So, in the Check Out Spots, we ask you for your ideas about "entertainment". What does this word mean for you?

We really hope you'll enjoy reading and using 'Entertainment'.

Susan Holden

contents

2 Check it out
3 It's festival time!
4 Festivals: more than the music
5 Behind the music
6 What strange music!
8 The story of a group: The Beatles
10 Where do films come from?
12 Music opens doors: The Amazon Youth Cello Choir
14 Music sells!
16 The story of a group: Franz Ferdinand
18 A recipe for making music
20 The (modern) circus is coming
21 The clowns' story
22 Do you know?
23 Projects
24 Topics chatrooms

TO THE **TOPICS** USERS

VOCABULARY You can find the key vocabulary for every article in the **WORD FILE** on that page. The pictures will also help you to guess the meaning in context. There is a summary of useful vocabulary on the **Check it out** page. Finally, you can use the *Macmillan Essential Dictionary* to consolidate the new vocabulary.

WEBSITES There is a list of useful website addresses on page 2. Remember that websites change. Be selective!

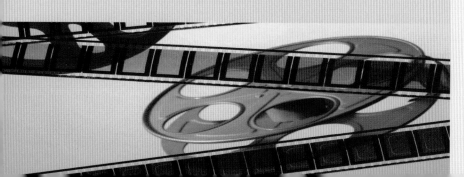

Check it out

Watching

Verbs
applaud	attend	cheer
clap	cry	laugh
listen	participate	watch

Places
auditorium	circle	orchestra 🇺🇸
seat	stalls 🇬🇧	ticket office

People
audience	critic	spectator

Some types of entertainment

ballet	cinema	circus
comedy	concert	dance
drama	film 🇬🇧	movie 🇺🇸
music	opera	play
theater 🇺🇸	theatre 🇬🇧	tragedy

Commenting

Positive
Bravo!	Encore!	exciting
fantastic	funny	great
moving	superb	wonderful

Neutral
not bad	O.K.	so-so

Negative
awful	Boo!	boring
disastrous	dull	terrible

Taking part

Verbs
act	compose	dance
film	perform	play
record	rehearse	sing

Places
cinema 🇬🇧	concert hall	movie theater 🇺🇸
platform	screen	stadium
stage	tent	theater

People
actor	artist	comedian
composer	conductor	dancer
designer	director	musician
performer	singer	writer

Sources and Resources

We consulted a lot of sources for 'Entertainment': people, books and the Internet. If you want to find out more about of the topics, here are some useful Internet sites.
All of them were "live" at the date of publication. Add your favourite sites and other useful resources.

Amazon Cello project: **www.acvapara.org**
The Beatles: **www.iamthebeatles.com** & **www.beatlesstory.com**
Franz Ferdinand: **www.franzferdinand.co.uk**
Films: **www.filmreview.com** & **www.imdb.com**
Festivals: **www.virtualfestivals.com** & **www.glastonburyfestivals.co.uk**
Vienna Vegetable Orchestra: **www.vegetableorchestra.**

IT'S FESTIVAL TIME!

Woodstock!
Glastonbury!
Rock in the Park!
Rock in Rio!

In parts of the world, summer means "festival time". It's an opportunity to hear famous bands and singers "live" - to be part of a big event, with several thousand other people. Also to dress up (or down), to dance, to do crazy things.

Some music festivals are only for one day. Others go on for several days. They are usually out of doors. They often have "tent cities", where people can sleep. There are places to buy food and drink. They become a "special world" for those few days.

For the organisers, there are huge practical problems, of course. What about the traffic? Are there enough places for cars? Will there be too much noise? Will the police cooperate? And what about insurance for accidents? Are there enough toilets and showers for several thousand people? What is the best price for the tickets? They mustn't be too expensive for young people, but they must cover the festival costs.

And – especially in some countries – will it rain?

Find out about some different kinds of festivals in your area. What's special about them?

WORD FILE

bungee-jumping	Jumping from a high place with a rubber rope so that you do not hit the ground.
cover the costs (v)	To have enough money to pay the expenses.
dress down (v)	To wear relaxed clothes.
dress up (v)	To wear formal clothes.
insurance	The money you pay as a precaution against loss or damage.
live	Not recorded.
out of doors	In the open air.
several	More than two, but not a great quantity.
shower	A metal object with small holes. The water comes through these to wash your body.
talk	Informal lecture about a topic.

🇺🇸 favorite
organizer
program
specialized
theater

🇬🇧 favourite
organiser
programme
specialised
theatre

The biggest festivals often contain many different types of music. Jazz, reggae, country, electric, folk, blues, alternative – you can find all your favourite music styles on the programme. Other events are very specialised. Perhaps they only have one kind of classical music, or one style of folk music. Some festivals also include talks, or theatre, or clowns, or events like bungee-jumping.

Festivals: more than the music

Glastonbury 2004

Festivals are for fun, but many of them have a serious side, too. They raise money for charity. The big British festival, Glastonbury, helps three charities: Greenpeace, Oxfam and WaterAid. The charities take part in the festival in different ways.

In summer 2004, Oxfam provided 1300 volunteers for the Festival. They acted as guides and checked tickets. They also directed the traffic, and helped with emergencies. Above all, they helped to create a good atmosphere – and, of course, they also had a good time!

WaterAid looked after the showers and toilet facilities – and promoted its work to provide clean drinking water in Third World Countries.

Greenpeace also provided showers – solar-assisted, of course – and an organic café. There were places to exercise: a climbing wall and a skateboard area. It also organised discussions about the effects of GM crops. After the event, it helped the organisers to clear up the environment. In return, each charity received US$200-300,000 from the organisers – and they recruited lots of new members.

Rock in Rio-Lisboa

The organisers of the Rock in Rio Festival want to build a better world. They use some of the money for social projects. They help young people to go to school and to study. At the Rock in Rio-Lisboa Festival in 2004, there was a big tent for meetings and debates. People discussed subjects like youth, social differences, technology, the environment and world peace. There was a special 3-minutes' silence to promote world peace. Paul McCartney was there (see page 8), and so was Gilberto Gil, Brazil's Minister for Culture at the time (see page 5). After the silence, Gil played "Imagine" with Rui Veloso, the Portuguese rock star.

Music festivals are great opportunities for listening and looking. They encourage you to think about issues and to help to find solutions. And their memory can last for years. Woodstock is a name that people still recognise all over the world.

WORD FILE	
charity	An organisation that collects money to help people.
clear up (v)	To make a place tidy again.
G.M. crops	Genetically modified plants for food.
issue	Topic that people discuss.
provide (v)	To make something available.
raise money (v)	To collect money.
solar-assisted	Powered by the sun.
toilet facilities	Places to wash.
volunteer	A person who works for no money.
youth	Young people.

🇺🇸 organize (v) program recognize (v)	🇬🇧 organise (v) programme recognise (v)

Behind

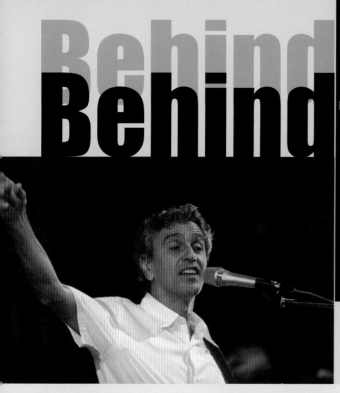

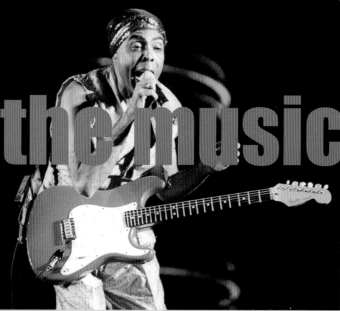

Behind the music

These two singers are famous all over the world – especially, of course, in their home country, Brazil.

Caetano Veloso

His albums sell in huge quantities. He's very popular. His fans adore him. But how many people know more than this? In fact, both Veloso and Gil were part of a famous musical movement in Brazil, "Tropicalismo". Their music was, at the time, revolutionary. Both of them had to leave their country, and go into exile.

Today, you can find Veloso at literary festivals, like FLIP (Festa Literária Internacional de Paraty), as well as at music festivals. He often speaks about the black community. He wants Brazil to take a leading part in discussions about racial problems.

Gilberto Gil

He is currently the Brazilian Minister for Culture. Oh, and also a singer and musician who regularly performs in top-level concerts, attracting huge and enthusiastic crowds. For example, he played and sang at the Rock in Rio-Lisboa Festival in 2004 (see page 4).

You often see newspaper photos of Gil. These may show him at work in Paris or New York, at the United Nations or in government meetings, or at a writers' conference. Or they may present him as a musician, doing a different kind of work on-stage in Rio de Janeiro or Salvador.

It must be difficult to do two jobs. Well, Gil has a lot of energy. What's the secret? Perhaps his diet helps him. He follows a macrobiotic diet: lots of vegetables and fruit. And he exercises. He says, "In the culture in which I grew up, I used to go to bed at three, four, five in the morning, and sleep late. Now I have had to adapt to exactly the reverse life. It's about good physical form."

Exile in London

Where did they go, these two singers from Bahia, in the semi-tropical northeast of Brazil? To cold, foggy, rainy London! Luckily, they could work there. They even wrote and sang in English. Veloso's "London, London" is one of the best expressions of the Portuguese word "saudade" (homesickness or nostalgia), the sadness people feel when they are far from their home, their family and their friends.

In fact, England in the 1960s wasn't such a bad place for musicians. It was the time of the groups like the Rolling Stones and the Beatles (see page 8). Music was in the air. "Swinging London" was famous for the shortest miniskirts, the wildest fashions, and the coolest music. There were hippies there, too, and psychedelic music and art. There was also West Indian music (London already had a big Caribbean community), so Gil and Veloso heard Bob Marley and rap music.

When they returned to Brazil, they took all these influences back with them.

Music and society

Today, rap is still important for Gil. He encourages young rappers from the "favelas" (slums) to contact other musicians and songwriters. He explains to them how rap came out of the African tradition – and still provides a connection between these cultures. Musical culture is dynamic: it has a past and a future, as well as a present.

WORD FILE	
exile	When a person has to live outside his or her country for political reasons.
hippy	A person who is against war, has long hair and often supports non-violence.
homesickness	Wanting to be at home again.
nostalgia	Thoughts about happy times in the past.
psychedelic	Very brightly coloured.
rap	Words with a strong rhythm and poetry - and (sometimes) music.
rapper	A person who performs rap music.

 colored   coloured

and social activities. What ideas influenced their music?

UT SPOT.

WHAT STRANGE MUSIC!
The First Vienna

Organic music... this is the latest thing in some European cities. It's experimental. It makes something out of nothing. It encourages people to think. And it sounds (and tastes) good! Are you puzzled? Here are a few facts.

Who's in the orchestra?

In 1998, a small group of artists got together to work on a new project. They wanted to experiment with musical sounds. They decided to use vegetables as musical instruments.

How many people are in the group?

At present, there are eight or nine musicians, one sound technician – and a cook. You see, at the end of the concert, the cook makes soup out of the vegetables. And the audience can taste it!

What kind of music do they play?

All kinds. They invent their own music. They play African music, and classical European styles. And now they sometimes include electronic music, too. They play these kinds of music on their vegetable instruments.

Which vegetables do they use?

It depends on what's in the market! The most useful and common ones are carrots, cucumbers and peppers. Then there are pumpkins (they make a sound like drums). They use cabbages (their leaves squeak), and onions (their skin makes a special sound). Tomatoes are good, too (OK, so they're really fruit...).

How can the audience hear the sounds?

The musicians have to make the sounds louder, so amplification is very important. That's why the sound technician is a key member of the orchestra. They use different types of microphones to amplify the sounds. This is very delicate and important work.

Here is part of their score for "Automate".

Copyright F.VO.

How do they make the instruments?

First of all, the musicians go to the market and buy really top quality, fresh vegetables. To make the musical instruments, they use sharp knives and electric hand-drills. For example, this is how they make a carrot flute. First of all, they choose a firm, straight carrot. Then they cut off the two ends. After this, they drill a hole through it, from top to bottom. They cut out a small, square hole, about two centimetres from one end of the carrot. Finally, they blow across the flute, like across a glass bottle. It makes a sound!

If they want to make different sounds, they cut more holes. They can then change the pitch with their fingers.

Vegetable Orchestra

Any other ideas?

The most complicated instrument is the "cucophone". They hollow out a 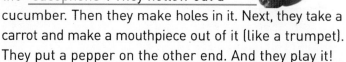 cucumber. Then they make holes in it. Next, they take a carrot and make a mouthpiece out of it (like a trumpet). They put a pepper on the other end. And they play it!

Is it difficult to play?

No, because people do not have any preconceptions about these instruments. Everybody knows what sound a violin or a guitar makes. Nobody knows what a "cucophone" sounds like. You feel free. You can invent your own sound. And when you play with colleagues, in a group, you can have fun. And you begin to look at other everyday things in a different way. Chairs, knives... What kind of sounds do they make?

And afterwards?

Don't forget the soup!
Which is better – the soup or the music?!

Is this serious?

Well, they give two or three concerts every month. And they have made two CDs. Of course, people make some "normal" instruments out of organic materials. Maracas, for example. And bamboo pipes. Perhaps this is just a very extreme example.

WORD FILE	
amplification	A way to make a sound louder.
amplify (v)	To make a sound louder.
blow (v)	To push air out of your mouth.
drill (v)	To make a hole with a metal instrument.
experimental	Using new ideas.
hand-drill	A machine to make holes in something solid.
hole	A circular space in the surface of an object.
hollow out (v)	To remove the inside of something.
mouthpiece	The part of a musical instrument that goes into your mouth.
organic	Natural and without chemicals.
pitch	How high or low a sound is.
preconception	An idea about something before you have much information.
sharp	With an edge that can cut objects easily.
sound technician	The person responsible for the technical part of a concert or recording.
squeak (v)	To make a high vocal noise.
🇺🇸 centimeter	🇬🇧 centimetre

Serious? You decide!

The story of a group:

People called them "the Fab Four". When they arrived for their first U.S. tour, 5000 fans were waiting at J.F.K. Airport in New York. Over 70 million viewers watched their first U.S. performance on coast-to-coast T.V. One of their songs, "I want to hold your hand" went to the No. 1 spot in the U.S. charts. And people of all ages still know and listen to their music all over the world. "Yesterday", "Imagine", "Hey Jude" and so many others.

NOTE: There are no dates in this article. When did the Beatles begin? When did the group break up? Any ideas? (Answers on Page 24.)

George, John, Ringo and Paul – The Beatles

How did it begin?

Liverpool is a big, industrial city in the north-west of England. It's a port, at the mouth of the River Mersey. From here, big ships used to travel around the world, to North and South America, Australia and New Zealand, Africa, Asia. Emigrants sailed from here to new lives across the Atlantic Ocean. The city is famous for this – and for a special kind of music: the Mersey Sound.

There were lots of bands and singers in Liverpool, but one group became more famous than all the others: The Beatles. How did this group begin?

A school group

When he was 16, John Lennon had a group called The Quarrymen. He invited Paul McCartney to join it. Then Paul invited one of his school friends, George Harrison. They changed the name of the group to "The Silver Beatles". Very soon, they changed it again to... The Beatles.

After he left school, John went to Liverpool Art College, and a friend from there, Stuart (Stu) Sutcliffe, joined the group. They added a drummer, Pete Best. The group went to the port of Hamburg, in Germany, to play in clubs there. It was a tough life, in a tough city – but they learned a lot. When they went back to Liverpool two years later, they were a really good group. Unfortunately, Stu Sutcliffe died suddenly.

Discovery!

The group played at the Cavern Club in Liverpool more than 270 times. This was the home of rock'n'roll in the city – hot, dark, crowded – and exciting. The Beatles attracted big crowds. One night, the owner of a local record store, Brian Epstein, went to hear them. He was impressed. He decided to get them a recording contract.

This wasn't so easy. All the recording companies were in London – and nobody knew Brian Epstein there. Finally, E.M.I. showed some interest. They asked the group to go to their recording studio in North London, in Abbey Road. Here they recorded their first hit, "Love Me Do". It went to Number 1 in the U.K. charts. They were on their way! At this time, a new drummer joined the group in place of Pete Best. His name was Richard Starkey, but he changed it to Ringo Starr.

The Beatles

Abbey Road

The Abbey Road Studio became famous. Here the Beatles worked with the producer George Martin. Over the next five years, albums such as "Help", "Revolver", "Sergeant Peppers Lonely Hearts Club Band" and "Abbey Road" sold millions of copies all over the world. Tracks like "Yesterday", "All You Need is Love" and "Yellow Submarine" became famous.

The Beatles made films, too: "A Hard Day's Night", "Help" and "The Yellow Submarine". They experimented with different styles of music. The hippy, psychedelic world attracted them. They went to India and learned about eastern philosophy. John Lennon met and married a Japanese artist, Yoko Ono. Each member of the group was developing in a different way.

Then, suddenly, the Beatles broke up. The world was shocked!

WORD FILE

break up (v)	To stop working as a group.
chart	A list of the CDs that have sold most copies.
coast-to-coast T.V.	T.V. programmes that you can see all over the U.S.
emigrant	A person who goes to live in a different country.
fab	From "fabulous". Very good.
fan	An enthusiastic supporter.
hippy	A person who is against war, has long hair and often supports non-violence.
impressed (to be)	To admire something or somebody.
massive	Very large or heavy.
No. 1 spot	The CD which has sold the most copies.
producer	The person who organises a recording session.
psychedelic	Very brightly coloured.
sail (v)	To travel by boat or ship.
singalong	When people get together and sing songs for fun.
track	One section on a CD.

🇺🇸	🇬🇧
colored	coloured
favorite	favourite
movie	film
organize (v)	organise (v)
program	programme

How many Beatles songs or albums do you know? Ask some people of different ages what their favourite Beatles hit was.

What happened to them all?

John Lennon went to live in New York. Several years later, he was murdered.

George Harrison visited India many times. He wrote more hits, but he died from cancer.

Ringo Starr acted in some movies and made a few more recordings. His son, Zak, is a drummer too. He plays with the group Oasis.

Paul McCartney still continues to write music and to sing. Recently, he did a world tour. The audiences were full of old and new fans. A 15-year-old went to listen. He wasn't sure that he liked the Beatles. Afterwards, he said, "He launched into a string of amazing songs, beginning with 'Back in the USSR'... He conducted massive singalongs to 'Hey Jude' and 'Yellow Submarine'". The boy was impressed. And the Beatles have a new fan!

Paul also sang "Back in the USSR" at an open-air concert in Russia, in St Petersburg. There were thousands of fans there. And in summer 2004 he performed at the Glastonbury Music Festival. Again, a big success. Sales of the album of Beatles hits doubled after that.

What's next? How long will the Beatles story continue? Who knows!

THE PAST

Writer: Homer
Date: About 1000 B.C.
Title: The Iliad

Subject: The story of the Trojan War. Paris, Prince of Troy, ran away with Helen, the wife of the Greek King of Sparta. A huge Greek army then sailed across the Aegean Sea to the city of Troy, to bring her back. This city had strong, high walls. The Greek army was enormous – but they couldn't get into the city.

The war went on for ten years. There were many battles between the Greeks and the Trojans. Famous soldiers like Achilles and Hector were killed. Finally, the Greeks succeeded in entering Troy. One of their leaders, Odysseus, suggested a trick. The Greeks made a big wooden horse which they left outside the city gates. Then they pretended to sail back to Greece.

The Trojans thought that the horse was a present from the Greeks. They pulled it into their city. They believed that they had won the war. But that night, secret doors in the horse opened. Odysseus and his soldiers climbed out. The Greeks were in Troy! They killed most of the inhabitants and destroyed the city.

Comment: The Iliad, and its sequel, The Odyssey, survived for more than 3000 years! People in many countries know the stories. Other writers and poets all over the world used the same   characters and the stories. Good stories never die.

Identify another movie with an interesting story behind it. Is it still relevant today?

THE PRESENT

Writer: David Benioff
Date: 2004 A.D.
Title: Troy

Subject: The story of the Trojan War. […] The war went on for ten years. [...] and destroyed the city.
As you see, it's exactly the same story!

Comment: The latest film, "Troy", is a big international project. It was filmed in Mexico, Malta and the U.K. The singers are Bulgarian. The director is German. The actors come from many different countries. The film, like the original story, is now travelling around the world.

That's international entertainment!

WORD FILE

battle	A big fight with a lot of soldiers.
run away (v)	To leave a place quickly.
sequel	The next part of a story.
survive (v)	To escape death.
trick	A very clever idea.

 movie
traveling

 film
travelling

A JOURNEY

THE BOOK

Author: Ernesto Guevara
Date: 1952/3
Title: Notas de Viaje (The Motorcycle Diaries) published in Argentina.

Subject: This diary is about a motorcycle trip. Ernesto was studying medicine, and his friend Alberto Granada was a young biochemist. They were both interested in leprosy. They decided to go on a journey: to ride on a motorcycle from Buenos Aires in Argentina to North America. This was a huge distance. The route went over snowy mountains, through the desert, and across huge rivers and lakes. In fact, they didn't get to North America.

They took Alberto's old motorcycle, La Poderosa II (The Powerful Woman). They crossed the Andes to Chile.

However, it broke down before they arrived at Valparaiso, on the coast. They had to leave it behind. After that, they hitched lifts on lorries, or walked. They went north, up into the Atacama Desert. After that, they went into Peru, Colombia and Venezuela. Ernesto wrote a diary, and Alberto took photos.

On their journey, they met a lot of very poor people. They saw illness, hunger, poverty and injustice. They spent two weeks in a Peruvian leper colony. For both of them, the trip opened their eyes to social problems and inequality.

Comment: After his trip, Ernesto Guevara graduated as a doctor. He continued to travel in Latin America. As a result of seeing poverty at first-hand, he became interested in revolutionary politics. He went to Cuba with Fidel Castro, and was the doctor for the guerrilla fighters. They called him "Che", and so he became "Che" Guevara. An icon was born.

THE ICON

For the next ten years, "Che" Guevara lived and worked in Cuba. Alberto went to live there too. Later, Che joined the revolutionary movement in Bolivia – and was killed. His face became a symbol for students and revolutionaries.

THE FILM

Director: Walter Salles. He also directed the international hit "Central Station" (Central do Brasil).
Date: 2004. (The film received The Cannes Special Prize for "high artistic quality" in France.)
Title: The Motorcycle Diaries (Diários de Motocicleta).

Comment: It is based on Guevara's Diary. The director also talked to Alberto, who was 81 when they made the film. He still remembers his friend. "To get to know Che Guevara more fully, and not just through his speeches and political life, you also need to know something about his background, how he grew up, his travels."

Salles worked on the film for five years. Robert Redford encouraged him. Like the Diary, it's a film about a journey, an adventure story. We see the students crossing the Andes, travelling on a raft, swimming across the Amazon at night. Just two students, having fun. We see the serious side, too: the visit to the leper colony. And we know that one of them will become famous.

The language of the movie is Spanish, with subtitles. The actors are from Argentina, Chile, Mexico and Peru. The director is Brazilian. Another story which will travel around the world.

WORD FILE

background	The ideas or facts behind something.
first-hand	Personal (when you see or do things yourself).
hitch (v)	To travel by car without paying.
icon	A very famous person who represents an idea.
injustice	Things which are not fair.
leper colony	A place where people with leprosy live to be away from others.
leprosy	A serious illness which affects skin, nerves and bones.

🇺🇸 movie	🇬🇧 film
traveling	travelling
truck	lorry

MUSIC OPENS DOORS:
THE AMAZON YOUTH CELLO CHOIR

THE AMAZON

What do you immediately think of?
Brazil. The rainforest... and... umm...
Yes. And cellos?
Cellos? No...
**And an orchestra – playing music
by Villa Lobos, and Bach, and more
modern composers?**
No, of course not!
Well, you're going to have a surprise...

THE PLACE

The state of Pará is in the far north of Brazil. The huge River
Amazon runs through it. Its capital city, Belém, is on the delta,
near the equator. It has a hot, wet, tropical climate – and,
of course, the Brazilian rainforest is famous all over the world.
Brazil is a huge country, and the north is a long way from the big
cities of São Paulo and Rio de Janeiro. A lot of people in the south
do not know much about it. As one teenager from the group said,
"They think there are wild animals in the streets here!".
A hundred years ago, Belém was a rich city, because it exported
rubber from the Amazon area all over the world. Students from other parts of
the state still come to study here. However, not all of them have the opportunity
to have a good education. In fact, it's a surprising place to find a cello orchestra,
especially one with an international reputation!

WORD FILE	
be determined (v)	To have strong ideas about what to do.
broadcast (v)	To put a programme on the radio.
contemplate (v)	To think about something.
dedication	Spending a lot of time and energy on a project.
disciplined	Well organised.
export (v)	To sell things outside your country.
full-sized	The same size as the original object.
import (v)	To bring things into your country to sell.
innovation	A new idea.
reputation	The things you are known for.
self-confident	Feeling sure of your ability.
tenacity	Continuing even when there are problems.

🇺🇸	🇬🇧
organized	organised
practice (v)	practise (v)
program	programme
traveled	travelled
traveling	travelling

THE PEOPLE

Aureo DeFreitas was born in the state of Pará, and went to secondary school
in Belém. There, he had a very good music teacher – and began to study the cello.
He continued his music studies in the U.S., at the University of Missouri-Columbia.
When he returned to Brazil, he began to teach the cello in Belém. He welcomed
a lot of students to his classes and he persuaded the music school to lend them cellos
to play on. He began to experiment with new methods to teach large classes.

More and more students decided to join the group. Their ages were from 10 to 18. The students were
very enthusiastic about the instrument. "It's like the human voice", one of them said. At one time,
85 of them were learning it. Playing together in the orchestra, they made good friends. They could
discuss their problems – school, family, money, boyfriends, girlfriends – everything.

Find some other projects in which
art or music "opens doors".

CHECKOUT SPOT

THE PROBLEMS

It wasn't easy for them, however. Cellos are big instruments – and expensive. They are difficult to carry around. Not many families could afford to buy one. As well as their normal school work, the students had to practise a lot. And many of them had to travel for long distances on buses.

Some of the players were quite young – and small. Normally, young players play smaller-sized instruments. But all *their* cellos were full-sized – made for adults. The kids had to carry their instruments on the bus. They usually had to stand at the back, as the cellos were too big to fit into a seat. They were afraid their instruments might hit something, and break. As well as this, some of the players lived in dangerous parts of the city. One of the parents was a taxi-driver – and he was a great help!

But they were determined to succeed. The Amazon Youth Cello Choir was born.

OVERCOMING PROBLEMS

Finding cellos to play was one problem. Travelling to the city for lessons was another. Also, they needed a place to practise. Sometimes they could use part of a church. But it was difficult. It's very hot and humid in northern Brazil. That's not good for cellos. And, of course, it's very hard to learn and practise when you are hot and sticky.

SUCCESS!

In spite of all the problems, the group worked really hard. They met and practised whenever they could. After a few years, they had enough confidence to give some concerts. They wanted to perform in front of some visitors from the BBC and from the Patek Philippe International magazine. They played in the grand old Teatro da Paz in Belém. It was a magical occasion for the audience. They all listened to the music of Villa Lobos and other classical composers. This was played beautifully by the young musicians, who were self-confident, disciplined and creative.

A LUCKY MEETING

Mark Rickards, a radio producer from the BBC in Britain, was travelling in Brazil. He heard about the orchestra, and thought it was a great project. So he decided to make a radio programme about them. He interviewed Aureo, and some of the musicians. He described the group, their problems, and their successes. They played music by Bach, Haydn and Vivaldi. He recorded all this, and the programme, "Music from the Rainforest", was broadcast in February 2003.

"These children have shown incredible dedication and tenacity – the difficulties of learning to play the cello in the Amazon is hard to contemplate."

He made another programme about them one year later in February 2004, and donated two cellos to the group.

PLAYING TO THE WORLD

These radio programmes were a great success. Some concert organisers in the Netherlands heard them. They decided to fly the orchestra to Europe. A lot of radio listeners in Britain were very enthusiastic about the project, too. They wanted to help the young musicians. Some of them wrote to the BBC and offered money to buy instruments. There was enough money to buy four more cellos, a hard case and some music.

The group played at a concert in Amsterdam. It was the first time many of them had travelled outside the Amazon region.

THE FUTURE

People in the U.S., Britain and the Netherlands are continuing to offer help and support. In Brazil, Aureo DeFreitas' teaching method – using the more advanced students to teach the others – is attracting a lot of attention. He is now working on his PhD in Music Education at the University of South Carolina in the U.S. His academic studies are sponsored by CAPES, an important educational institution in Brazil. He goes back to Belém twice a year to work with the group. They also keep in touch through the Internet.

Some of the young musicians will be able to study at music colleges in Brazil and abroad. Best of all, their music, the inspiration of their teacher, and their hard work, have provided them with great satisfaction.

The state of Pará is becoming well known for innovation in music education – not just for the rainforest! Music *can* open doors.

NOTE: It's not just in the north of Brazil - David Chew, a British cellist in Rio de Janeiro, has helped them to give several concerts in that state.

music

Ever seen this guy?

He's George Frederick Handel. He was a German, though he went to live in England. He was born in 1685 and died in 1759. Over 300 years ago. He composed a lot of music: "The Messiah" (remember the Halleluiah Chorus?), "The Water Music"...

What's that got to do with us, today?

Wait! I'm sure you know what these are!
Sure – they're jeans!
But they're not 300 years old... They're modern!

Well, that's the link. Read on...

The new Levi's campaign

Levi's jeans launched a new advertising campaign in Europe. Like most ads, these used music. And what did the advertising agency choose? Handel's "Sarabande in D Minor".

Handel wrote this piece for a single harpsichord. Levi's rearranged it for a full orchestra. It's very dramatic – just like the ad. In it, two people do amazing things. They crash through walls, run up trees, and then jump into a huge night sky. Wearing Levi's, of course!

Levi's have used classical or old pieces of music for their ads in the past. And these pieces often become hits. They are recorded in an exciting way, and so they seem modern. They introduce teens to classical music AND they sell things. Handel may soon be "Top of the Pops" all over Europe!

sells!

Artistic and commercial - two different worlds?

Most bands and groups are really happy to record music for ads. People associate their name with specific products – mobiles, jeans, and so on. This helps them to become famous. It also makes it easier to sell their other things – CDs and tickets for their concerts. Of course, they prefer to provide music for "cool" products. And there can be ethical problems. Will a vegetarian group provide music for a hamburger ad?

Words or emotions?

In the past, most ads used "jingles" – special words and music written about the product. But now these soundtracks are more like film music. They express a mood, which reinforces the visual message. Often, people remember the music, and want to know who performed it - and who wrote it. Then the sales of other music by the same composer usually increase dramatically.

Film music – the new classics?

The sales of film music can be enormous. Soundtracks like "Gladiator", "Apocalypse Now" and "Titanic" are really popular. And their success can be worldwide, too, just like the films. "Gladiator" sold more than a million copies.

For some composers, writing film soundtracks compensates for the difficulty of making money from their "serious" work. But what's the difference? Pop music, dance music, classical... Perhaps it's just music.

WORD FILE

advertising agency	A company that organises advertising.
campaign	A series of ads for a product.
compose (v)	To make up music.
crash (v)	To go into something with a lot of force.
harpsichord	A musical instrument like a small piano.
launch (v)	To start a new activity or project.
link	Connection.
mood	The way you feel (happy, sad, etc.).
orchestra	A large group of musicians.
rearrange (v)	To put things in a different way.
soundtrack	The music played during a film or a T.V. programme.

 movie
organize (v)
program

 film
organise (v)
programme

Who are they?

Are they new?

So why are they important?

A band from Glasgow, in Scotland.

Quite new. They got together in 2001.

Well, people think they're going to have a big future. They're very popular in the U.S. We thought you might like to be some of the first people to know about them!

O.K. Tell us something about them...

There are four of them:

The drummer: Paul Thomson. He worked at Glasgow School of Art.

The bass player: Bob Hardy. He was a student there.

The singer: Alexander (Alex) Kapranos. He was studying English at university, but he had lots of friends at the art school.

The guitarist: Nick McCarthy. He used to live in Germany, but he moved to Glasgow.

James Goulden

What kind of music did they decide to play?

They felt that post-rock music was too serious.

> "We want people to go away from the gigs humming the tunes that we were singing."

They wanted to make good music for dancing. Their first gig was at a fashion show at Glasgow Art School. Some female art students asked them to provide music for it.

Their first eight singles

Darts of Pleasure - Released September 2003.

Take Me Out - Released 12 January 2004.

Went to no. 3 in the U.K. charts.

Matinee - 19 January 2004. > 8

Michael - 16 August 2004. > 17

This Ffire - 8 November 2004. > 8

Do You Want To - 19 September 2005. > 4

Walk Away - 5 December 2005. > 13

The Fallen - 13 February 2006.

Part of a track from the album
Franz Ferdinand

```
"You see her
You can't touch her
You hear her
You can't hold her
You want her
You can't have her
You want to
But she won't let you..."
```
Copyright Franz Ferdinand/Domino Records.

Their albums in 2004 and 2005

Franz Ferdinand - Released 9 February 2004. > 3 *

You Could Have It So Much Better - Released 3 October 2005. > 1

*NOTE: Guess where this CD was mastered? In a famous studio in North London... Yes - good guess! Abbey Road.

Ferdinand

James Goulden

What will happen to the group in the future?
Visit their website (www.franzferdinand.co.uk) and follow their progress.

What people say about them

"They're a charismatic bunch of guys. They have just got what it takes."

(Peter Ellen, Chief Executive of Fopp Records)

"We are really excited about them."

(Julian Marshall, Group News Editor of New Music Express)

What the group say

"We're always scribbling away. Writing songs is thrilling and fun, that's why we do all this stuff."

(Alex Kapranos)

"The band is the grandest possible adventure you can go on with your friends."

(AK)

WORD FILE	
bunch of guys	A group of men.
charismatic	Making people want to listen to you.
fashion show	A parade of new clothes.
gig	A public performance of music.
hum (v)	To make music without opening your mouth.
post-rock music	Music that develops from rock'n'roll.
release (v)	To put a CD on sale.
scribble (v)	To write quickly.
stuff	A collection of things.
thrilling	Very exciting.
tune	A piece of music.

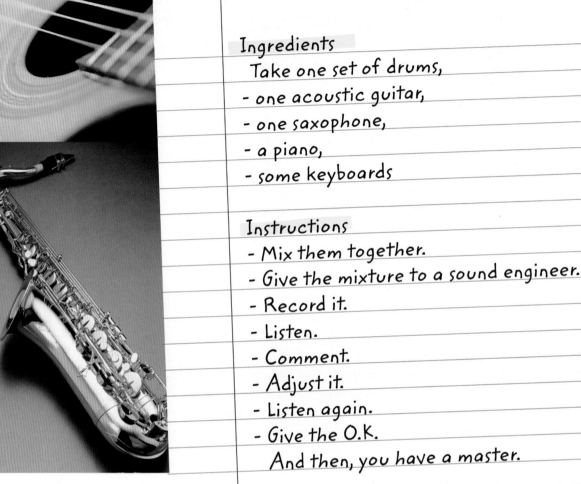

Ingredients

Take one set of drums,
- one acoustic guitar,
- one saxophone,
- a piano,
- some keyboards

Instructions
- Mix them together.
- Give the mixture to a sound engineer.
- Record it.
- Listen.
- Comment.
- Adjust it.
- Listen again.
- Give the O.K.
   And then, you have a master.

It's just like cooking!

Do you ever wonder how musicians "make" a track? Some of them do it completely digitally, of course. But some musicians use real instruments, and then the sound engineer mixes the sound.

It's a little like putting the pieces of a jigsaw puzzle together. Or cooking a dish: you choose the ingredients, decide on the quantities, and mix them together.

We asked a group of musicians to tell us what they did. They were working on a track called "Annabel's Theme".

The musicians: What instruments do they play?

There were four musicians at the recording session: Dave, Pete Z, Simon N and Pete W. They all play different instruments. Dave is a drummer. Pete Z plays bass guitar and saxophone. Simon N is a guitarist. And Pete W plays the piano, and two different synthesised keyboards. He is also the composer. There is one more important person: the sound engineer, Simon B.

WORD FILE	
adjust (v)	To change in small ways to make it better.
composer	A person who writes music.
digitally	Storing music electronically by numbers.
electronically	To do something using electronics.
emotional	With a lot of feeling.
experiment (v)	To do something in a new way.
foundation	The part under all the other parts.
improvise (v)	To make music that is not written down.
intro	The first part (introduction).
mix (v)	To combine several things.
synthesized keyboard	An electronic keyboard.
take off (v)	To be successful.
track	One section of a CD.
vary (v)	To do things in different ways.

🇺🇸 favorite
synthesized

🇬🇧 favourite
synthesised

MAKING MUSIC

The instruments: How do they sound different?

Like the drummer, the bass player provides the rhythm. Pete Z feels he's the "bridge" between the drummer and the other musicians. He also works closely with the pianist. He likes to be part of the "foundation" of the music. However, it's fun to provide the melody, too. And the saxophone is ideal for this! It's an emotional instrument. It can add a different kind of sound. The acoustic guitarist works closely with the drummer. He takes the rhythm and plays with it.

The process: What did the musicians do?

First of all, the musicians decided on the kind of sound that they wanted. Then Pete W sat down at the piano. He began to experiment with an intro, just improvising. The others listened, and made comments, "and we just took off from there, whatever felt right".

The drummer said he "just played what came naturally". He provides the basic rhythm, so he must be a good musician.

The group used the synthesisers to add different sounds. Again, Pete W tried different things, and they all commented.

Enter the engineer: What did he do?

When they had a sound that they all liked, it was the engineer's turn. It was time to record. He put a mike (microphone) near every instrument (in fact, there were 14 mikes around the drums). Each mike was connected to a different track on the recording deck. For "Annabel's Theme", they used 21 tracks. The engineer could vary the sound of each track. They all listened, and made comments. They decided that the sax solo should begin quiet, and then get louder. So that was done electronically.

The result

When you hear the final result, it's difficult to believe that there are so many different tracks in it. If it's good, you only hear the total sound. It's just like tasting a good dish!

Look at the text on the covers of some of your favourite CDs. What instruments do they list? How many people are *not* musicians? What are their jobs?

CHECKOUT SPOT

THE (MODERN) CIRCUS IS COMING

There is something special about a circus! They're different from other forms of entertainment – theatre, films, concerts. They appear one day – and next week, they disappear! One day, you notice a poster. Then, perhaps, you see a big, multicoloured tent going up on a piece of wasteland. It's difficult not to feel excited.

The components

What are the traditional parts of a circus? First of all, there's the tent, the "big top". Inside here, anything is possible! And it's better than a film, or T.V. – it's "live".

People

Then there are the people. Clowns, of course (see page 21). Jugglers throw balls into the air – and catch them. Perhaps the trapeze artists are the best. They swing about high up in the air, and fly through it like birds. They do incredible things high up above your head. Is there a safety net? Will they fall?

Animals

There are usually animals, too, of course. Horses dance on their back legs, and obey commands. They are so intelligent! Is this cruel? Well, they are not asked to do anything abnormal.

Wild animals - that's a different matter. In the old circuses, there were elephants and sea lions. They balanced on balls and did tricks. There were even lions, tigers and snakes. This has begun to change, because many people feel that it is cruel. The animals had to do unnatural things. They often lived in cramped conditions. Now, of course, people can see wild animals in their natural habitats on T.V. – they are not so "exotic" any more. In fact, more and more circuses now have no wild animals. One of the first of these new kinds of circus was the Grand Magic Circus in France.

WORD FILE	
cramped	Without space.
cruel	Very unkind.
graduate	A person who completes a university course.
juggler	A person who throws many balls into the air.
live	Performance in front of an audience.
multicoloured	With many colours.
obey (v)	To do what someone tells you to do.
safety net	A net to catch people if they fall.
swing about (v)	To move backwards and forwards through the air.
wasteland	An empty area of land in a city.

🇺🇸 color	🇬🇧 colour
multicolored	multicoloured
movie	film
theater	theatre

Modern developments

In the past, there used to be "family circuses": all the members of the family worked in it. Sometimes there were several generations of one family. Today, young circus performers want to experiment. They find different ways to communicate and to express their emotions.

In France, circuses are very popular these days. There, circus is an art form, like theatre, music, dance and singing. There are over 200 special circus schools. The students learn to juggle and to fly on the trapeze. They also learn to play musical instruments and dance. These are useful physical skills like swimming or tennis, which are good for the body.

The graduates of these modern circus schools join the famous companies, and travel all over the world. Two of the most successful young French groups are Anomalie (toured in Vietnam and Brazil), Zingaro (a big success in New York). Pierrot Bidon, one of the members of Archaos, is training a new generation of circus entertainers in Brazil.

Circuses now attract new audiences: not just children. The circus is old – but it's modern too!

THE CLOWNS' STORY

Universal and Eternal

There's one necessary ingredient in any circus: the clowns. They tell jokes, they do funny things, and the crowd laughs. But some people say that clowns are sad. They paint their faces, but underneath, they see the absurdity of life.

"What a clown!"

There are clowns in most cultures. If one of our friends is good at telling jokes, we often say "He's a bit of a clown". If someone is fooling around in class, the teacher may say "Stop clowning around!". So – clowns are universal. Where do they come from?

Clowns everywhere

Well, there were clowns in Ancient Egypt. And in Ancient China. When Pisarro went to Mexico in 1520 A.D., he found clowns there like those in Europe. In some cultures, clowns had an important social or religious role. They could even cure illnesses.

Harlequin and friends

The first "modern" clowns began in the 16th century in Italy, in the Commedia Dell'Arte theatre. In these plays, there were usually three kinds of funny character:

- a clever male servant
- a stupid male servant
- a clever female servant

Shakespeare used some of these clown characters in his plays.

Harlequin (Arlecchino) developed from the clever male servant. He played tricks on other people – and on his master. He sang and danced.

White-faced clowns

The white-faced clown developed from the "stupid" servant. This kind of clown made people laugh in the circus. A favorite "act" of this clown was to try to get onto a horse. He always fell off! Joseph Grimaldi was a famous "white-faced" clown. He used to sing funny songs – and singing clowns still make people laugh.

The funny (or sad) "little man" character is also a type of clown. Think of Charlie Chaplin: big shoes, an enormous coat, and a big hat.

A serious profession

There are lots of modern clowns. They're serious about their profession, too. There's an Association of Clowns in the U.S. and in Britain. In London, there's a Clowns Museum. Different kinds of clowns find their way into festivals (see pages 4 & 5) everywhere. There are comedy shows on the radio, and on T.V. Some of the jokes may be different – but many are the same. And people still laugh at them.

WORD FILE

character	The role an actor performs in a play, film, etc.
clown around (v)	To do silly things to make people laugh.
fool around (v)	To act in a silly way for fun.
joke	Something funny you say to make people laugh.
servant	Someone who does jobs for a person or a family.
trick	Something you do to make someone believe in something false.

🇺🇸 favorite theater   🇬🇧 favourite theatre

The big question: **Are clowns happy** or sad? **What do you think?**

How many different types of clowns exist in your culture? Do you find them funny?

CHECKOUT SPOT

Quiz

Do you know?

(Answers on page 24.)

1. MOVIE PRIZES

Match the Film Festivals and the top prizes.

1	Venice	☐	Oscar
2	Cannes	☐	Golden Bear
3	Berlin	☐	Golden Lion
4	Hollywood	☐	Golden Palm
5	Gramado	☐	People's Choice
6	Toronto	☐	Kikito

2. WATCHING AND DOING

Entertainment equivalents: find the pairs here.
Follow the model.

Watching

1 Going to a concert.
2 Watching a play.
3 Seeing a great film.
4 Laughing at a T.V. cartoon.
5 Watching a parade.
6 Listening to an exciting story.
7 Visiting a museum.
8 Tuning in to your favourite radio channel.

Doing

☐ Telling a joke.
☐ Making a video.
☐ Dressing up and taking part in a festival.
☐ Inventing a good story.
☐ Performing in a play.
☐ Being a D.J. on a student radio programme.
☐ 1 Playing live music.
☐ Making your own personal collection.

3. QUOTATIONS

Here are famous quotations about entertainment. Choose the right word and complete them.

STAGE	MUST	NIGHT	SHOW

1 There's no business like ●●● business.
2 The show ●●● go on.
3 All the world's a ●●●.
4 It'll be all right on the ●●●!

4. HARRY POTTER

Put these titles in order of publication (1-6).

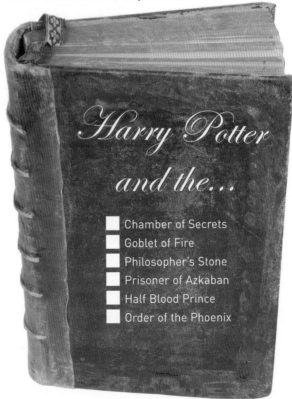

Harry Potter and the...

☐ Chamber of Secrets
☐ Goblet of Fire
☐ Philosopher's Stone
☐ Prisoner of Azkaban
☐ Half Blood Prince
☐ Order of the Phoenix

Projects

COVER DESIGN

The topic of this Topics title is **Entertainment**. Look at our front cover. Is this good for the topic? Design your own cover to express your ideas about the topic.

1

MUSIC GROUPS

Choose a new music group. Find out as much as you can about them. Their personal lives and their music. Present your information in the best form (poster, audio, etc.).

4

FESTIVALS CALENDAR

Research festivals in your region or country. Divide them into categories, e.g. music, theatre, film. You may want to subdivide these categories, e.g. into different styles of music. Then design a year's calendar for them.

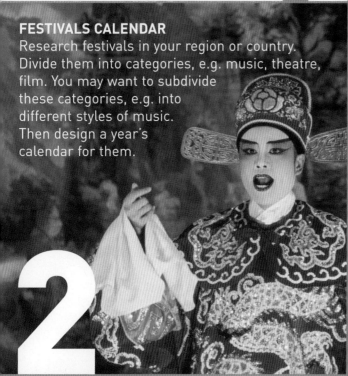

2

ENTERTAINMENT: YOUR CHOICE!

Choose your favorite topics and pictures to design a new Entertainment Magazine. Work with some friends and plan the contents. If you have time, make a real one.

5

FILM PROJECT

Choose a book to turn into a film. Decide what the "message" will be. Choose your "dream" actors and director. Present your ideas on a poster or website for your film.

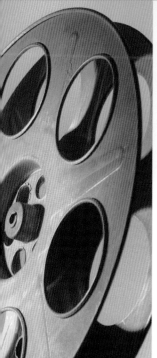

3

PERSONAL ENTERTAINMENT

Do a survey among your friends. What are their favourite forms of entertainment? Are these "watching", or "doing"? Find a way to present the information in pictures, graphs or tables.

6

 Collect all the info from your Checkout Spots. Choose the best ones, and present them in an **Entertainment Exhibition.**

Topics chatrooms

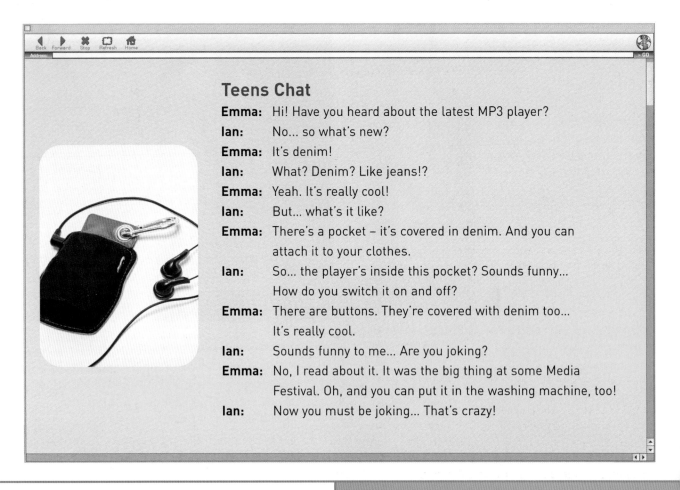

Teens Chat

Emma: Hi! Have you heard about the latest MP3 player?

Ian: No... so what's new?

Emma: It's denim!

Ian: What? Denim? Like jeans!?

Emma: Yeah. It's really cool!

Ian: But... what's it like?

Emma: There's a pocket – it's covered in denim. And you can attach it to your clothes.

Ian: So... the player's inside this pocket? Sounds funny... How do you switch it on and off?

Emma: There are buttons. They're covered with denim too... It's really cool.

Ian: Sounds funny to me... Are you joking?

Emma: No, I read about it. It was the big thing at some Media Festival. Oh, and you can put it in the washing machine, too!

Ian: Now you must be joking... That's crazy!

Can you believe it?

People have festivals for all sort of things. In some places, bread is really important. They even have special days to celebrate it. People dress up, they play music, have competitions - and they make, and eat, lots of bread. Can you guess which country this festival is in? The answer is in Facts Check (don't cheat!).

Facts Check

Answers

Page 8:
The Beatles made their first evening appearance in 1961 and broke up as a group in 1970.

Page 22:

1. MOVIE PRIZES
4/3/1/2/6/5

2. WATCHING AND DOING
4/3/5/6/2/8/1/7

3. QUOTATIONS
1) show; 2) must; 3) stage; 4) night

4. HARRY POTTER
2/4/1/3/6/5

Page 24:
Can you believe it?   France

GOODBYE!
That's the end of 'Entertainment'.
We hope you've enjoyed it. See you in the next one.

Susan Holden